'Let ot[...]
jolting [...]
confide,
Or in the leaky
Boat the *Thames*
divide'

JOHN GAY
Born 1685, Barnstaple, England
Died 1732, London, England

Trivia: or, the Art of Walking the Streets of London
was first published in 1716.

JOHN GAY IN PENGUIN CLASSICS
The Beggar's Opera

JOHN GAY

Trivia:

or, the Art of Walking the Streets of London

PENGUIN BOOKS

PENGUIN CLASSICS

UK | USA | Canada | Ireland | Australia
India | New Zealand | South Africa

Penguin Classics is part of the Penguin Random House group of companies
whose addresses can be found at global.penguinrandomhouse.com.

First edition first published in Penguin Classics 2016
001

Set in 9/12.4 pt Baskerville 10 Pro
Typeset by Jouve (UK), Milton Keynes
Printed in Great Britain by Clays Ltd, St Ives plc

A CIP catalogue record for this book is available from the British Library

ISBN: 978-0-241-25229-1

www.greenpenguin.co.uk

Penguin Random House is committed to a
sustainable future for our business, our readers
and our planet. This book is made from Forest
Stewardship Council® certified paper.

Quo te Mœri pedes? An, quo via ducit, in Urbem?

Virg.

Book I.

OF THE IMPLEMENTS FOR WALKING THE STREETS, AND SIGNS OF THE WEATHER.

Through winter streets to steer your course aright,
How to walk clean by day, and safe by night,
How jostling crouds, with prudence, to decline,
When to assert the wall, and when resign,
I sing: thou *Trivia*, goddess, aid my song,
Thro' spacious streets conduct thy bard along;
By thee transported, I securely stray
Where winding alleys lead the doubtful way,
The silent court, and op'ning square explore,
And long perplexing lanes untrod before.
To pave thy realm, and smooth the broken ways,
Earth from her womb a flinty tribute pays;
For thee, the sturdy paver thumps the ground,
Whilst ev'ry stroke his lab'ring lungs resound;
For thee, the scavinger bids kennels glide
Within their bounds, and heaps of dirt subside.
My youthful bosom burns with thirst of fame,
From the great theme to build a glorious name,
To tread in paths to ancient bards unknown,
And bind my temples with a *civic* crown;
But more, my country's love demands the lays,
My country's be the profit, mine the praise.

When the *black youth* at chosen stands rejoice,
And 'clean your shoes' resounds from ev'ry voice;
Who late their miry sides stage-coaches show,
And their stiff horses thro' the Town move slow;
When all the *Mall* in leafy ruin lies,
And damsels first renew their oyster cries:

Of shoes. Then let the prudent walker shoes provide,
Not of the *Spanish* or *Morocco* hide;
The wooden heel may raise the dancer's bound,
And with the scallop'd top his step be crown'd:
Let firm, well-hammer'd soles protect thy feet
Thro' freezing snows, and rains, and soaking sleet.
Should the big laste extend the shoe too wide,
Each stone will wrench th' unwary step aside:
The sudden turn may stretch the swelling vein,
Thy cracking joint unhinge, or ankle sprain;
And when too short the modish shoes are worn,
You'll judge the seasons by your shooting corn.

Of coats. Nor should it prove thy less important care,
To chuse a proper coat for winter's wear.
Now in thy trunk thy *d'oily* habit fold,
The silken drugget ill can fence the cold;
The frieze's spongy nap is soak'd with rain,
And show'rs soon drench the camlet's cockled grain.
True *Witney** broad-cloath with it's shag unshorn,
Unpierc'd is in the lasting tempest worn:

*   *A town in* Oxfordshire.

Be this the horse-man's fence; for who would wear
Amid the Town the spoils of *Russia*'s bear?
Within the *roquelaure*'s clasp thy hands are pent,
Hands, that stretch'd forth invading harms prevent.
Let the loop'd *bavaroy* the fop embrace,
Or his deep cloak be spatter'd o'er with lace.
That garment best the winter's rage defends,
Whose shapeless form in ample plaits depends;
By various names* in various counties known,
Yet held in all the true *surtout* alone:
Be thine of *Kersey* firm, though small the cost,
Then brave unwet the rain, unchill'd the frost.

If the strong cane support thy walking hand,   *Of canes.*
Chairmen no longer shall the wall command;
Ev'n sturdy car-men shall thy nod obey,
And rattling coaches stop to make thee way:
This shall direct thy cautious tread aright,
Though not one glaring lamp enliven night.
Let beaus their canes with amber tipt produce,
Be theirs for empty show, but thine for use.
In gilded chariots while they loll at ease,
And lazily insure a life's disease;
While softer chairs the tawdry load convey
To Court, to *White*'s,† assemblies, or the play;
Rosie-complexion'd health thy steps attends,
And exercise thy lasting youth defends.

*   A Joseph, *a wrap-rascal, &c.*
†   White's *chocolate-house in St.* James's

Imprudent men heav'ns choicest gifts prophane.
Thus some beneath their arm support the cane;
The dirty point oft checks the careless pace,
And miry spots thy clean cravat disgrace:
O! may I never such misfortune meet,
May no such vicious walkers croud the street,
May Providence o'er-shade me with her wings,
While the bold Muse experienc'd dangers sings.

Not that I wander from my native home,
And tempting perils foreign cities roam.
Let *Paris* be the theme of *Gallia*'s muse,
Where slav'ry treads the streets in wooden shoes;
Nor do I rove in *Belgia*'s frozen clime,
And teach the clumsy boor to skate in rhyme,
Where, if the warmer clouds in rain descend,
No miry ways industrious steps offend,
The rushing flood from sloping pavements pours,
And blackens the canals with dirty show'rs.
Let others *Naples*' smoother streets rehearse,
And with proud *Roman* structures grace their verse,
Where frequent murders wake the night with groans,
And blood in purple torrents dies the stones;
Nor shall the muse through narrow *Venice* stray,
Where *gondolas* their painted oars display.
O happy streets to rumbling wheels unknown,
No carts, no coaches shake the floating town!
Thus was of old *Britannia*'s city bless'd,
E'er pride and luxury her sons possess'd;
Coaches and chariots yet unfashion'd lay,

Nor late invented chairs perplex'd the way:
Then the proud lady trip'd along the Town,
And tuck'd up petticoats secur'd her gown,
Her rosie cheek with distant visits glow'd
And exercise unartful charms bestow'd;
But since in braided gold her foot is bound,
And a long trailing manteau sweeps the ground,
Her shoe disdains the street; the lazy fair,
With narrow step affects a limping air.
Now gaudy pride corrupts the lavish age,
And the streets flame with glaring equipage;
The tricking gamester insolently rides,
With *Loves* and *Graces* on his chariots sides;
In sawcy state the griping broker sits,
And laughs at honesty, and trudging wits;
For you, O honest men, these useful lays
The Muse prepares; I seek no other praise.

When sleep is first disturb'd by morning cries; *Of the weather.*
From sure prognosticks learn to know the skies,
Lest you of rheums and coughs at night complain;
Surpriz'd in dreary fogs, or driving rain.
When suffocating mists obscure the morn,
Let thy worst wig, long us'd to storms, be worn;
This knows the powder'd footman, and with care,
Beneath his flapping hat, secures his hair.
Be thou, for ev'ry season, justly drest,
Nor brave the piercing frost with open breast;
And when the bursting clouds a deluge pour,
Let thy *surtout* defend the drenching show'r.

Signs of cold weather.

    The changing weather certain signs reveal.
E'er winter sheds her snow, or frosts congeal,
You'll see the coals in brighter flame aspire,
And sulphur tinge with blue the rising fire:
Your tender shins the scorching heat decline,
And at the dearth of coals the poor repine;
Before her kitchen hearth, the nodding dame
In flannel mantle wrapt, enjoys the flame;
Hov'ring, upon her feeble knees she bends,
And all around the grateful warmth ascends.

Signs of fair weather.

    Nor do less certain signs the Town advise,
Of milder weather, and serener skies.
The ladies gayly dres'd, the *Mall* adorn
With various dyes, and paint the sunny morn;
The wanton fawns with frisking pleasure range,
And chirping sparrows* greet the welcome change:
Not that their minds with greater skill are fraught,
Endu'd by instinct, or by reason taught,
The seasons operate on every breast;
'Tis hence that fawns are brisk, and ladies drest.
When on his box the nodding coachman snores,
And dreams of fancy'd fares; when tavern doors
The chairmen idly croud; then ne'er refuse
To trust thy busy steps in thinner shoes.

---

*   *Haud equidem credo quia sit divinitus illis, Ingenium, aut*
    rerum fator prudential major. Virg. Georg. I.

But when the swinging signs your ears offend   *Signs of*
With creaking noise, then rainy floods impend;   *rainy*
Soon shall the kennels swell with rapid streams,   *weather.*
And rush in muddy torrents to the *Thames*.
The bookseller, whose shop's an open square,
Foresees the tempest, and with early care
Of learning strips the rails; the rowing crew
To tempt a fare, cloath all their tilts in blue:
On hosier's poles depending stockings ty'd,
Flag with the slacken'd gale, from side to side;
Church-monuments foretell the changing air;
Then *Niobe* dissolves into a tear,
And sweats with secret grief; you'll hear the sounds
Of whistling winds, e'er kennels break their bounds;
Ungrateful odours common sewers diffuse,
And dropping vaults distil unwholesom dews,
E'er the tiles rattle with the smoaking show'r,
And spouts on heedless men their torrents pour.

All superstition from thy breast repel.   *Superstition*
Let cred'lous boys, and prattling nurses tell,   *to be avoided.*
How, if the festival of *Paul* be clear,
Plenty from lib'ral horn shall strow the year;
When the dark skies dissolve in snows or rain,
The lab'ring hind shall yoke the steer in vain;
But if the threatning winds in tempests roar,
Then war shall bathe her wasteful sword in gore.
How, if on *Swithin*'s feast the welkin lours,
And ev'ry penthouse streams with hasty show'rs,

Twice twenty days shall clouds their fleeces drain,
And wash the pavements with incessant rain.
Let not such vulgar tales debase thy mind;
Nor *Paul* nor *Swithin* rule the clouds and wind.

If you the precepts of the Muse despise,
And slight the faithful warnings of the skies,
Others you'll see, when all the town's afloat,
Wrapt in th' embraces of a *kersey* coat,
Or double-button'd freize; their guarded feet
Defie the muddy dangers of the street,
While you, with hat unloop'd, the fury dread
Of spouts high-streaming, and with cautious tread
Shun ev'ry dashing pool, or idly stop,
To seek the kind protection of a shop.
But bus'ness summons; now with hasty scud
You jostle for the wall, the spatter'd mud
Hides all thy hose behind; in vain you scow'r,
Thy wig, alas! uncurl'd, admits the show'r.
So fierce *Alecto*'s snaky tresses fell,
When *Orpheus* charm'd the rig'rous pow'rs of hell.
Or thus hung *Glaucus*' beard, with briny dew
Clotted and strait, when first his am'rous view
Surpris'd the bathing fair; the frighted maid
Now stands a rock, transform'd by *Circe*'s aid.

Implements proper for female walkers.

Good housewives all the winter's rage despise,
Defended by the riding-hood's disguise;
Or underneath th' *umbrella*'s oily shed,
Safe thro' the wet on clinking pattens tread.

Let Persian dames th' *umbrella*'s ribs display,
To guard their beauties from the sunny ray;
Or sweating slaves support the shady load,
When eastern monarchs shew their state abroad;
Britain in winter only knows its aid,
To guard from chilly show'rs the walking maid.
But, O! forget not, Muse, the *patten*'s praise,
That female implement shall grace thy lays;
Say from what art divine th' invention came,
And from its origine deduce the name.

Where *Lincoln* wide extends her fenny soil,   *An episode of*
A goodly yeoman liv'd grown white with toil;   *the invention*
One only daughter bless'd his nuptial bed,   *of pattens.*
Who from her infant hand the poultry fed:
Martha (her careful mother's name) she bore,
But now her careful mother was no more.
Whilst on her father's knee the damsel play'd,
Patty he fondly call'd the smiling maid;
As years increas'd, her ruddy beauty grew,
And *Patty*'s fame o'er all the village flew.

Soon as the gray-ey'd morning streaks the skies,
And in the doubtful day the woodcock flies,
Her cleanly pail the pretty housewife bears,
And singing to the distant field repairs:
And when the plains with ev'ning dews are spread,
The milky burthen smokes upon her head.
Deep, thro' a miry lane she pick'd her way,
Above her ankle rose the chalky clay.

   Vulcan, by chance the bloomy maiden spies,
With innocence and beauty in her eyes,
He saw, he lov'd; for yet he ne'er had known
Sweet innocence and beauty meet in one.
Ah *Mulciber*! recall thy nuptial vows,
Think on the graces of thy *Paphian* spouse,
Think how her eyes dart inexhausted charms,
And canst thou leave her bed for *Patty*'s arms?

   The *Lemnian* Pow'r forsakes the realms above,
His bosom glowing with terrestrial love:
Far in the lane, a lonely hut he found,
No tenant ventur'd on th' unwholesome ground.
Here smokes his forge, he bares his sinewy arm,
And early strokes the sounding anvil warm;
Around his shop the steely sparkles flew,
As for the steed he shap'd the bending shoe.

   When blue-ey'd *Patty* near his window came,
His anvil rests, his forge forgets to flame.
To hear his soothing tales, she feigns delays;
What woman can resist the force of praise?

   At first she coyly ev'ry kiss withstood,
And all her cheek was flush'd with modest blood:
With headless nails he now surrounds her shoes,
To save her steps from rains and piercing dews;
She lik'd his soothing tales, his presents wore,
And granted kisses, but would grant no more.

Yet winter chill'd her feet, with cold she pines,
And on her cheek the fading rose declines;
No more her humid eyes their lustre boast,
And in hoarse sounds her melting voice is lost.

This *Vulcan* saw, and in his heav'nly thought,
A new machine mechanick fancy wrought,
Above the mire her shelter'd steps to raise,
And bear her safely through the wintry ways.
Strait the new engine on his anvil glows,
And the pale virgin on the patten rose.
No more her lungs are shook with drooping rheums,
And on her cheek reviving beauty blooms.
The god obtain'd his suit, though flatt'ry fail,
Presents with female virtue must prevail.
The patten now supports each frugal dame,
Which from the blue-ey'd *Patty* takes the name.

Book II.

OF WALKING THE STREETS BY DAY.

Thus far the Muse has trac'd in useful lays,
The proper implements for wintry ways;
Has taught the Walker, with judicious eyes,
To read the various warnings of the skies.
Now venture, Muse, from home to range the Town,
And for the publick safety risque thy own.

The morning. For ease and for dispatch, the morning's best:
No tides of passengers the street molest.
You'll see a draggled damsel, here and there,
From *Billingsgate* her fishy traffick bear;
On doors the sallow milk-maid chalks her gains;
Ah! how unlike the milk-maid of the plains!
Before proud gates attending asses bray,
Or arrogate with solemn pace the way;
These grave physicians with their milky chear,
The love-sick maid, and dwindling beau repair;
Here rows of drummers stand in martial file,
And with their vellom-thunder shake the pile,
To greet the new-made bride. Are sounds like these,
The proper prelude to a state of peace?
Now industry awakes her busy sons,
Full charg'd with news the breathless hawker runs:
Shops open, coaches roll, carts shake the ground,
And all the streets with passing cries resound.

If cloath'd in black, you tread the busy Town,
Or if distinguish'd by the rev'rend gown,
Three trades avoid; oft' in the mingling press,
The *barber*'s apron soils the sable dress;
Shun the *perfumer*'s touch with cautious eye,
Nor let the *baker*'s step advance too nigh:
Ye walkers too that youthful colours wear,
Three sullying trades avoid with equal care;
The little *chimney-sweeper* skulks along,
And marks with sooty stains the heedless throng;
When *small-coal* murmurs in the hoarser throat,
From smutty dangers guard thy threaten'd coat:
The *dust-man*'s cart offends thy cloaths and eyes,
When through a street a cloud of ashes flies;
But whether black, or lighter dyes are worn,
The *chandler*'s basket, on his shoulder born,
With tallow spots thy coat; resign the way,
To shun the surly *butcher*'s greasy tray,
Butchers, whose hands are dy'd with blood's foul stain,
And always foremost in the hangman's train.

What trades prejudical to walkers.

Let due civilities be strictly paid.
The wall surrender to the hooded maid;
Nor let thy sturdy elbow's hasty rage
Jostle the feeble steps of trembling age:
And when the porter bends beneath his load,
And pants for breath; clear thou the crouded road.
But above all, the groping blind direct,
And from the pressing throng the lame protect.

To whom to give the wall.

You'll sometimes meet a fop, of nicest tread,
Whose mantling peruke veils his empty head,
At ev'ry step he dreads the wall to lose,
And risques, to save a coach, his red-heel'd shoes;
Him, like the *miller*, pass with caution by,
Lest from his shoulder clouds of powder fly.

To whom to refuse the wall.

But when the bully, with assuming pace,
Cocks his broad hat, edg'd round with tarnish'd lace,
Yield not the way; defie his strutting pride,
And thrust him to the muddy kennel's side;
He never turns again, nor dares oppose,
But mutters coward curses as he goes.

Of whom to enquire the way.

If drawn by bus'ness to a street unknown,
Let the sworn porter point thee through the Town;
Be sure observe the signs, for signs remain,
Like faithful land-marks to the walking train.
Seek not from prentices to learn the way,
Those fabling boys will turn thy steps astray;
Ask the grave tradesman to direct thee right,
He ne'er deceives, but when he profits by't.

Where fam'd St. *Giles*'s ancient limits spread,
An inrail'd column rears its lofty head,
Here to sev'n streets, sev'n dials count the day,
And from each other count the circling ray.
Here oft the peasant, with enquiring face,
Bewilder'd, trudges on from place to place;
He dwells on ev'ry sign, with stupid gaze,

Enters the narrow alley's doubtful maze,
Tries ev'ry winding court and street in vain,
And doubles o'er his weary steps again.
Thus hardy *Theseus*, with intrepid feet,
Travers'd the dang'rous labyrinth of *Crete*;
But still the wandring passes forc'd his stay,
Till *Ariadne*'s clue unwinds the way.
But do not thou, like that bold chief, confide
Thy ventrous footsteps to a female guide;
She'll lead thee, with delusive smiles along,
Dive in thy fob, and drop thee in the throng.

When waggish boys the stunted besom ply, *Useful precepts.*
To rid the slabby pavement; pass not by
E'er thou hast held their hands; some heedless flirt
Will over-spread thy calves with spatt'ring dirt.
Where porters hogsheads roll from carts aslope,
Or brewers down steep cellars stretch the rope,
Where counted billets are by carmen tost;
Stay thy rash steps, and walk without the post.

What though the gath'ring mire thy feet besmear,
The voice of industry is always near.
Hark! the boy calls thee to his destin'd stand,
And the shoe shines beneath his oily hand.
Here let the Muse, fatigu'd amid the throng,
Adorn her precepts with digressive song;
Of shirtless youths the secret rise to trace,
And show the parent of the sable race.

Like mortal man, great *Jove* (grown fond of
    change)
Of old was wont this nether world to range
To seek amours; the vice the monarch lov'd
Soon through the wise etherial court improv'd,
And ev'n the proudest goddess now and then
Would lodge a night among the sons of men;
To vulgar deities descends the fashion,
Each, like her betters, had her earthly passion.
Then *Cloacina** (goddess of the tide
Whose sable streams beneath the City glide)
Indulg'd the modish flame; the Town she rov'd,
A mortal scavenger she saw, she lov'd;
The muddy spots that dry'd upon his face,
Like female patches, heighten'd ev'ry grace:
She gaz'd; she sigh'd. For love can beauties spy
In what seems faults to ev'ry common eye.

Now had the watchman walk'd his second round;
When *Cloacina* hears the rumbling sound
Of her brown lover's cart, for well she knows
That pleasing thunder: swift the goddess rose,
And through the streets pursu'd the distant noise,
Her bosom panting with expected joys.

---

*   Cloacina *was a goddess whose image* Tatius (*a king of the*
    Sabines) *found in the common sewer, and not knowing what*
    goddess it was, he called it Cloacina, *from the place in which*
    it was found, and paid to it divine honours. Lactant 1.20.
    Minuc. Fel. Octo. p. 232.

With the night-wandring harlot's airs she past,
Brush'd near his side, and wanton glances cast;
In the black form of cinder-wench she came,
When love, the hour, the place had banish'd shame;
To the dark alley, arm in arm they move:
O may no link-boy interrupt their love!

When the pale moon had nine times fill'd
    her space,
The pregnant goddess (cautious of disgrace)
Descends to earth; but sought no midwife's aid,
Nor midst her anguish to *Lucina* pray'd;
No cheerful gossip wish'd the mother joy,
Alone, beneath a bulk, she dropt the boy.

The child through various risques in years
    improv'd,
At first a beggar's brat, compassion mov'd;
His infant tongue soon learnt the canting art,
Knew all the pray'rs and whines to touch the heart.

O happy unown'd youths, your limbs can bear
The scorching dog-star, and the winter's air,
While the rich infant, nurs'd with care and pain,
Thirsts with each heat, and coughs with ev'ry rain!

The goddess long had mark'd the child's distress,
And long had sought his suff'rings to redress;
She prays the gods to take the fondling's part,
To teach his hands some beneficial art

Practis'd in streets; the gods her suit allow'd,
And made him useful to the walking croud,
To cleanse the miry feet, and o'er the shoe
With nimble skill the glossy black renew.
Each power contributes to relieve the poor:
With the strong bristles of the mighty boar
Diana forms his brush; the god of day
A tripod gives, amid the crouded way
To raise the dirty foot, and ease his toil;
Kind *Neptune* fills his vase with fetid oil
Prest from th' enormous whale; the god of fire,
From whose dominion smoaky clouds aspire,
Among these gen'rous presents joins his part,
And aids with soot the new japanning art:
Pleas'd she receives the gifts; she downward glides,
Lights in *Fleet-ditch*, and shoots beneath the tides.

Now dawns the morn, the sturdy lad awakes,
Leaps from his stall, his tangled hair he shakes,
Then leaning o'er the rails, he musing stood,
And view'd below the black canal of mud,
Where common sewers a lulling murmur keep,
Whose torrents rush from *Holborn*'s fatal steep:
Pensive through idleness, tears flow'd apace,
Which eas'd his loaded heart, and wash'd his face;
At length he sighing cry'd, 'That boy was blest,
Whose infant lips have drain'd a mother's breast;
But happier far are those, (if such be known)
Whom both a father and a mother own:
But I, alas! hard Fortune's utmost scorn,

Who ne'er knew parent, was an orphan born!
Some boys are rich by birth beyond all wants,
Belov'd by uncles, and kind good old aunts;
When time comes round, a Christmas-box they bear,
And one day makes them rich for all the year.
Had I the precepts of a father learn'd,
Perhaps I then the coachman's fare had earn'd,
For lesser boys can drive; I thirsty stand
And see the double flaggon charge their hand,
See them puff off the froth, and gulp amain,
While with dry tongue I lick my lips in vain.'

While thus he fervent prays, the heaving tide
In widen'd circles beats on either side;
The goddess rose amid the inmost round,
With wither'd turnip tops her temples crown'd;
Low reach'd her dripping tresses, lank, and black
As the smooth jet, or glossy raven's back;
Around her waste a circling eel was twin'd,
Which bound her robe that hung in rags behind.
Now beck'ning to the boy; she thus begun,
'Thy prayers are granted; weep no more, my son:
Go thrive. At some frequented corner stand,
This brush I give thee, grasp it in thy hand,
Temper the soot within this vase of oil,
And let the little tripod aid thy toil;
On this methinks I see the walking crew
At thy request support the miry shoe,
The foot grows black that was with dirt imbrown'd,
And in thy pocket jingling halfpence sound.'

The goddess plunges swift beneath the flood,
And dashes all around her show'rs of mud:
The youth strait chose his post; the labour ply'd
Where branching streets from *Charing-cross* divide;
His treble voice resounds along the *Mews*,
And *White-hall* echoes—'Clean your honour's shoes.'

Like the sweet ballad, this amusing lay
Too long detains the Walker on his way;
While he attends, new dangers round him throng;
The busy City asks instructive song.

Where elevated o'er the gaping croud,
Clasp'd in the board the perjur'd head is bow'd,
Betimes retreat; here, thick as hailstones pour,
Turnips, and half-hatch'd eggs, (a mingled show'r)
Among the rabble rain: some random throw
May with the trickling yolk thy cheek o'erflow.

Of narrow streets.

Though expedition bids, yet never stray
Where no rang'd posts defend the rugged way.
Here laden carts with thundering waggons meet,
Wheels clash with wheels, and bar the narrow street;
The lashing whip resounds, the horses strain,
And blood in anguish bursts the swelling vein.
O barb'rous men, your cruel breasts assuage,
Why vent ye on the gen'rous steed your rage?
Does not his service earn your daily bread?
Your wives, your children, by his labours fed!
If, as the *Samian* taught, the soul revives,

And shifting seats, in other bodies lives;
Severe shall be the brutal coachman's change,
Doom'd, in a *Hackney* horse, the Town to range:
Carmen, transform'd the groaning load shall draw,
Whom other tyrants, with the lash, shall awe.

Who would of *Watling-street* the dangers share,
When the broad pavement of *Cheapside* is near?
Or who that rugged street* would traverse o'er,
That stretches, O *Fleet-ditch*, from thy black shore
To the *Tow'r*'s moated walls? Here steams ascend
That, in mix'd fumes, the wrinkled nose offend.
Where chandlers cauldrons boil, where fishy prey
Hide the wet stall, long absent from the sea;
And where the cleaver chops the heifer's spoil,
And where huge hogsheads sweat with trainy oil,
Thy breathing nostril hold; but how shall I
Pass, where in piles *Cornavian*† cheeses lye;
Cheese, that the table's closing rites denies,
And bids me with th'unwilling chaplain rise.

The most inconvenient streets to walkers.

O bear me to the paths of fair *Pall-mall*,
Safe are thy pavements, grateful is thy smell!
At distance, rolls along the gilded coach,
Nor sturdy carmen on thy walks encroach;
No lets would bar thy ways, were chairs deny'd,
The soft supports of laziness and pride;

The Pall-mall *celebrated.*

* Thames-street.
† Cheshire *anciently so called.*

Shops breathe perfume, thro' sashes ribbons glow,
The mutual arms of ladies, and the beau.
Yet still ev'n here, when rains the passage hide,
Oft the loose stone spirts up a muddy tide
Benath thy careless foot; and from on high,
Where masons mount the ladder, fragments fly;
Mortar, and crumbled lime in show'rs descend,
And o'er thy head destructive tiles impend.

The pleasure of walking through an alley

But sometimes let me leave the noisie roads,
And silent wander in the close abodes
Where wheels ne'er shake the ground; there pensive
stray,
In studious thought, the long uncrouded way.
Here I remark each walker's diff'rent face,
And in their look their various bus'ness trace.
The broker here his spacious beaver wears,
Upon his brow sit jealousies and cares;
Bent on some mortgage, to avoid reproach,
He seeks bye streets, and saves th' expensive coach.
Soft, at low doors, old letchers tap their cane,
For fair recluse, that travels *Drury-lane*.
Here roams uncomb'd, the lavish rake, to shun
His *Fleet-street* draper's everlasting dun.

Inconveniences that attend those who are unacquainted with the Town.

Careful observers, studious of the Town,
Shun the misfortunes that disgrace the clown.
Untempted, they contemn the juggler's feats,

Pass'd by the *Mews*, nor try the thimble's cheats.*
When drays bound high, they never cross behind,
Where bubbling yest is blown by gusts of wind:
And when up *Ludgate-hill* huge carts move slow,
Far from the straining steeds, securely go,
Whose dashing hoofs, behind them, fling the mire,
And mark, with muddy blots, the gazing 'squire.
The *Parthian* thus his jav'lin backward throws,
And as he flies, infests pursuing foes.

The thoughtless wits shall frequent forfeits pay,
Who 'gainst the centry's box discharge their tea.
Do thou some court, or secret corner seek,
Nor flush with shame the passing virgin's cheek.

Yet let me not descend to trivial song,
Nor vulgar circumstance my verse prolong;
Why should I teach the maid when torrents pour,
Her head to shelter from the sudden show'r?
Nature will best her ready hand inform,
With her spread petticoat to fence the storm.
Does not each walker know the warning sign,
When wisps of straw depend upon the twine
Cross the close street: that then the paver's art
Renews the ways, deny'd to coach and cart?
Who knows not, that the coachman lashing by,
Oft, with his flourish, cuts the heedless eye;

Precepts vulgarly known.

---

* *A cheat, commonly practic'd in the streets, with three thimbles
  and a little ball.*

23

And when he takes his stand, to wait a fare,
His horses foreheads shun the winter's air?
Nor will I roam, when summer's sultry rays
Parch the dry ground, and spread with dust the ways;
With whirling gusts, the rapid atoms rise,
Smoak o'er the pavement, and involve the skies.

Frosty weather.   Winter my theme confines; whose nitry wind
Shall crust the slabby mire, and kennels bind;
She bids the snow descend in slaky sheets,
And in her hoary mantle cloath the streets.
Let not the virgin tread these slipp'ry roads,
The gath'ring fleece the hollow patten loads;
But if thy footsteps slide with clotted frost,
Strike off the breaking balls agains the post.
On silent wheel the passing coaches roll;
Oft' look behind and ward the threatening pole.
In harden'd orbs the school-boy moulds the snow,
To mark the coachman with a dextrous throw.
Why do ye, boys, the kennel's surface spread,
To tempt with faithless pass the matron's tread?
How can ye laugh, to see the damsel spurn,
Sink in your frauds and her green stocking mourn?
At *White*'s, the harness'd chairman idly stands,
And swings, around his waste, his tingling hands:
The sempstress speeds to *'change* with red-tipt nose;
The *Belgian* stove beneath her footstool glows,
In half-whipt muslin needles useless lye,
And shuttle-cocks across the counter fly.

These sports warm harmless; why then will you prove,
Deluded maids, the dang'rous flame of love?

Where *Covent-garden*'s famous temple stands,
That boasts the work of *Jones*' immortal hands;
Columns, with plain magnificence appear,
And graceful porches lead along the square:
Here oft' my course I bend, when lo! from far,
I spy the furies of the foot-ball war:
The 'prentice quits his shop, to join the crew,
Encreasing crouds the flying game pursue.
Thus, as you roll the ball o'er snowy ground,
The gath'ring globe augments with ev'ry round;
But whither shall I run? the throng draws nigh,
The ball now skims the street, now soars on high;
The dextrous glazier strong returns the bound,
And jingling sashes on the penthouse sound.

The dangers of foot-ball.

O roving Muse, recall that wond'rous year,
When winter reigned in bleak *Britannia*'s air;
When hoary *Thames*, with frosted oziers crown'd,
Was three long moons in icy fetters bound.
The waterman, forlorn along the shore,
Pensive reclines upon his useless oar,
Sees harness'd steeds desert the stony Town;
And wander roads unstable, not their own:
Wheels o'er the harden'd waters smoothly glide,
And rase with whiten'd tracks the slipp'ry tide.
Here the fat cook piles high the blazing fire,

An episode of the great frost.

And scarce the spit can turn the steer entire.
Booths sudden hide the *Thames*, long streets appear,
And num'rous games proclaim the crouded fair.
So when a gen'ral bids the martial train
Spread their encampment o'er the spatious plain;
Thick-rising tents a canvas city build,
And the loud dice resound thro' all the field.

'Twas here the matron found a doleful fate:
In elegiac lay the woe relate,
Soft, as the breath of distant flutes, at hours,
When silent ev'ning closes up the flow'rs;
Lulling, as falling water's hollow noise;
Indulging grief, like *Philomela*'s voice.

Doll ev'ry day had walk'd these treach'rous roads;
Her neck grew warpt beneath autumnal loads
Of various fruit; she now a basket bore,
That head, alas! shall basket bear no more.
Each booth she frequent past, in quest of gain,
And boys with pleasure heard her shrilling strain.
Ah *Doll*! all mortals must resign their breath,
And industry it self submit to death!
The cracking crystal yields, she sinks, she dyes,
Her head, chopt off, from her lost shoulders flies:
Pippins she cry'd, but death her voice confounds,
And pip-pip-pip along the ice resounds.
So when the *Thracian* furies *Orpheus* tore,
And left his bleeding trunk deform'd with gore,

His sever'd head floats down the silver tide,
His yet warm tongue for his lost consort cry'd;
Eurydice, with quiv'ring voice, he mourn'd,
And *Heber*'s banks *Eurydice* return'd.

But now the western gale the flood unbinds,   *A thaw.*
And black'ning clouds move on with warmer winds,
The wooden Town its frail foundation leaves,
And *Thames*' full urn rolls down his plenteous waves:
From ev'ry penthouse streams the fleeting snow,
And with dissolving frost the pavements flow.

Experienc'd men, inur'd to city ways,   *How to know*
Need not the calendar to count their days.   *the days of*
When through the Town, with slow and solemn air,   *the week.*
Led by the nostril, walks the muzled bear;
Behind him moves majestically dull,
The pride of *Hockley-hole*, the surly bull;
Learn hence the periods of the week to name,
Mondays and *Thursdays* are the days of game.

When fishy stalls with double store are laid;
The golden-belly'd carp, the broad-finn'd maid,
Red-speckled trouts, the salmon's silver joul,
The jointed lobster, and unscaly soale,
And luscious 'scallops, to allure the tastes
Of rigid zealots to delicious fasts;
Wednesdays and *Fridays* you'll observe from hence,
Days, when our sires were doom'd to abstinence.

When dirty waters from balconies drop,
And dextrous damsels twirl the sprinkling mop,
And cleanse the spatter'd sash, and scrub the stairs,
Know *Saturday*'s conclusive morn appears.

Remarks on the cries of the Town.

Successive crys the season's change declare,
And mark the monthly progress of the year.
Hark, how the streets with treble voices ring,
To sell the bounteous product of the spring!
Sweet-smelling flow'rs, and elders early bud,
With nettle's tender shoots, to cleanse the blood:
And when *June*'s thunder cools the sultry skies,
Ev'n *Sundays* are prophan'd by mackrel cries.

Walnuts the *fruit'rer*'s hand, in autumn, stain,
Blue plumbs, and juicy pears augment his gain;
Next oranges the longing boys entice,
To trust their copper-fortunes to the dice.

Of Christmas.

When rosemary, and bays, the poet's crown,
Are bawl'd, in frequent cries, through all the Town,
Then judge the festival of *Christmas* near,
Christmas, the joyous period of the year.
Now with bright holly all your temples strow,
With laurel green, and sacred mistletoe.
Now, heav'n-born *Charity*, thy blessings shed;
Bid meagre want uprear her sickly head:
Bid shiv'ring limbs be warm; let plenty's bowle,
In humble roofs, make glad the needy soul.
See, see, the heav'n-born maid her blessings shed.

Lo! meagre want uprears her sickly head;
Cloath'd are the naked, and the needy glad,
While selfish avarice alone is sad.

Proud coaches pass, regardless of the moan,
Of infant orphans, and the widow's groan;
While charity still moves the walker's mind,
His lib'ral purse relieves the lame and blind.
Judiciously thy halfpence are bestow'd,
Where the laborious beggar sweeps the road
Whate'er you give, give ever at demand,
Nor let old-age long stretch his palsy'd hand.
Those who give late, are importun'd each day,
And still are teaz'd, because they still delay.
If e'er the miser durst his farthings spare,
He thinly spreads them through the publick square,
Where, all beside the rail, rang'd beggars lie,
And from each other catch the doleful cry;
With heav'n, for twopence, cheaply wipes his score,
Lifts up his eyes, and hasts to beggar more.

*Precepts of
charity.*

Where the brass knocker, wrapt in flannel band,
Forbids the thunder of the footman's hand;
Th' upholder, rueful harbinger of death
Waits, with impatience, for the dying breath;
As vultures, o'er a camp, with hov'ring flight,
Snuff up the carnage of the fight.
Here cans't thou pass, unmindful of a pray'r,
That heav'n in mercy may thy brother spare?

Come, *F*— sincere, experienc'd friend,
Thy briefs, thy deeds, and ev'n thy fees suspend;
Come, let us leave the *Temple*'s silent walls,
Me bus'ness to my distant lodging calls:
Through the long *Strand* together let us stray,
With thee conversing, i forget the way.
Behold that narrow street, which steep descends,
Whose building to the slimy shore extends;
Here *Arundell*'s fam'd structure rear'd its frame,
The street alone retains an empty name:
Where *Titian*'s glowing paint the canvas warm'd,
And *Raphael*'s fair design, with judgment, charm'd,
Now hangs the bell-man's song, and pasted here,
The colour'd prints of *Overton* appear.
Where statues breath'd, the work of *Phidias*' hands,
A wooden pump, or lonely watch-house stands.
There *Essex*'s stately pile adorn'd the shore,
There *Cecil*'s, *Bedford*'s, *Viller*'s, now no more.
Yet *Burlington*'s fair palace still remains;
Beauty within, without proportion reigns.
Beneath his eye declining art revives,
The wall with animated picture lives;
There *Hendel* strikes the strings, the melting strain
Transports the soul, and thrills through ev'ry vein;
There oft I enter (but with cleaner shoes)
For *Burlington*'s belov'd by ev'ry Muse.

The happiness of walkers.

O ye associate walkers, O my friends,
Upon your state what happiness attends!
What, though no coach to frequent visit rolls,

Nor for your shilling chairmen sling their poles;
Yet still your nerves rheumatic pains defye,
Nor lazy jaundice dulls your saffron eye;
No wasting cough discharges sounds of death,
Nor wheezing asthma heaves in vain for breath;
Nor from your restless couch is heard the groan
Of burning gout, or sedentary stone.
Let others in the jolting coach confide,
Or in the leaky boat the *Thames* divide;
Or, box'd within the chair, contemn the street,
And trust their safety to another's feet,
Still let me walk; for oft' the sudden gale
Ruffles the tide, and shifts the dang'rous sail,
Then shall the passenger, too late, deplore
The whelming billow, and the faithless oar;
The drunken chairman in the kennel spurns,
The glasses shatters, and his charge o'erturns.
Who can recount the coach's various harms?
The legs disjointed, and the broken arms?

I've seen a beau, in some ill-fated hour,
When o'er the stones choak'd kennels swell the show'r,
In gilded chariot loll; he with disdain
Views spatter'd passengers, all drenched in rain;
With mud fill'd high, the rumbling cart draws near,
Now rule thy prancing steeds, lac'd charioteer!
The *dustman* lashes on with spiteful rage,
His pond'rous spokes thy painted wheel engage,
Crush'd is thy pride, down falls the shrieking beau,
The slabby pavement crystal fragments strow,

Black floods of mire th' embroider'd coat disgrace,
And mud enwraps the honours of his face.
So when dread *Jove*, the son of *Phoebus* hurl'd,
Scarr'd with dark thunder, to the nether world;
The headstrong coursers tore the silver reins,
And the sun's beamy ruin gilds the plains.

If the pale walker pants with weak'ning ills,
His sickly hand is stor'd with friendly bills:
From hence, he learns the seventh-born doctor's fame,
From hence, he learns the cheapest tailor's name.

Shall the large mutton smoak upon your boards?
Such, *Newgate*'s copious market best affords;
Would'st though with mighty beef augment thy meal?
Seek *Leaden-hall*; St. *James*'s sends thee veal.
Thames-street gives cheeses; *Covent-garden* fruits;
Moor-fields old books; and *Monmouth-street* old suits.
Hence may'st thou well supply the wants of life,
Support thy family, and clothe thy wife.

Volumes, on shelter'd stalls, expanded lie,
And various science lures the learned eye;
The bending shelves with pond'rous scholiasts groan,
And deep divines to modern shops unknown:
Here, like a bee that on industrious wing,
Collects the various odours of the spring,
Walkers, at leisure, learning's flow'rs may spoil,
Nor watch the wasting of the midnight oil,
May morals snatch'd from *Plutarch*'s tatter'd page,

A mildew'd *Bacon*, or *Stagyra*'s sage.
Here saunt'ring 'prentices o'er *Otway* weep,
O'er *Congreve* smile, or over *d*—— sleep;
Pleas'd sempstresses the *Lock*'s fam'd *rape* unfold,
And *Squirts** read *Garth*, 'till *apozems* grow cold.

O *Lintott*, let my labours obvious lie,
Rang'd on thy stall, for ev'ry curious eye;
So shall the poor these precepts *gratis* know,
And to my verse their future safeties owe.

What walker shall his mean ambition fix,
On the false lustre of a coach and six?
Let the vain virgin, lur'd by glaring show,
Sigh for the liv'rys of th'embroider'd beau.

See, yon' bright chariot on its harness swing,
With *Flanders* mares, and on an arched spring,
That wretch, to gain an equipage and place,
Betray'd his sister to a lewd embrace.
This coach, that with the blazon'd 'scutcheon glows,
Vain of his unknown race the coxcomb shows.
Here the brib'd lawyer, sunk in velvet, sleeps;
The starving orphan, as he passes, weeps;
There flames a fool, begirt with tinselled slaves,
Who wastes the wealth of a whole race of knaves.
That other, with a clustering train behind,
Owes his new honours to a sordid mind.

---

* *The name of an apothecary's* boy *in the poem of* 'The Dispensary'.

This next in court-fidelity excels,
The publick rifles, and his country sells.
May the proud chariot never be my fate,
If purchas'd at so mean, so dear a rate;
O rather give me sweet content on foot,
Wrapt in my vertue, and a good *surtout*!

Book III.

OF WALKING THE STREETS BY NIGHT.

O *Trivia*, goddess, leave these low abodes,
And traverse o'er the wide ethereal roads,
Celestial queen, put on thy robes of light,
Now *Cynthia* nam'd, fair regent of the night.
At sight of thee, the villain sheaths his sword,
Nor scales the wall, to steal the wealthy hoard.
Oh! may thy silver lamp in Heav'n's high bow'r
Direct my footsteps in the midnight hour.

When night first bids the twinkling stars appear, *The evening.*
Or with her cloudy vest inwraps the air,
Then swarms the busy street; with caution tread,
Where the shop-windows falling threat thy head;
Now lab'rers home return, and join their strength
To bear the tott'ring plank, or ladder's length;
Still fix thy eyes intent upon the throng,
And as the passes open, wind along.

Where the fair columns of St. *Clement* stand, *Of the pass of*
Whose straiten'd bounds encroach upon the *Strand*; *St. Clements.*
Where the low penthouse bows the walker's head,
And the rough pavement wounds the yielding tread;
Where not a post protects the narrow space,
And strung in twines, combs dangle in thy face;
Summon at once thy courage, rouse thy care,

Stand firm, look back, be resolute, beware.
Forth issuing from steep lanes, the *collier*'s steeds
Drag the black load; another cart succeeds,
Team follows team, crouds heap'd on crouds appear,
And wait impatient, 'till the road grow clear.
Now all the pavement sounds with trampling feet,
And the mixt hurry barricades the street.
Entangled here, the waggon's lengthen'd team
Crack the tough harness; here a pond'rous beam
Lies over-turn'd athwart; for slaughter fed,
Here lowing bullocks raise their horned head.
Now oaths grow loud, with coaches coaches jar,
And the smart blow provokes the sturdy war;
From the high box they whirl the thong around,
And with the twining lash their shins resound:
Their rage ferments, more dang'rous wounds they try,
And the blood gushes down their painful eye.
And now on foot the frowning warriors light,
And with their pond'rous fists renew the fight;
Blow answers blow, their cheeks are 'smear'd
          with blood,
'Till down they fall, and grappling roll in mud.
So when two boars, in wild *ytene** bred,
Or on *Westphalia*'s fatt'ning chestnuts fed,
Gnash their sharp tusks, and rous'd with equal fire,
Dispute the reign of some luxurious mire;
In the black flood they wallow o'er and o'er,
'Till their arm'd jaws distill with foam and gore.

*   New Forest *in* Hampshire, *anciently so called.*

Of pick-pockets.

Where the mob gathers, swiftly shoot along,
Nor idly mingle in the noisy throng.
Lur'd by the silver hilt, amid the swarm,
The subtil artist will thy side disarm.
Nor is thy flaxen wig with safety worn;
High on the shoulder, in the basket born,
Lurks the sly boy; whose hand to rapine bred,
Plucks off the curling honours of the head.
Here dives the skulking thief, with practis'd slight,
And unfelt fingers make thy pocket light.
Where's now thy watch, with all its trinkets, flown?
And thy late snuff-box is no more thy own.
But lo! his bolder theftsome tradesman spies,
Swift from his prey the scudding lurcher flies;
Dext'rous he 'scapes the coach, with nimble bounds,
While ev'ry honest tongue '*Stop thief*' resounds.
So speeds the wily fox, alarm'd by fear,
Who lately filch'd the turkey's callow care;
Hounds following hounds, grow louder as he flies,
And injur'd tenants joyn the hunter's cries.
Breathless he stumbling falls: ill-fated boy!
Why did not honest work thy youth employ?
Seiz'd by rough hands, he's dragg'd amid the rout,
And stretch'd beneath the pump's incessant spout:
Or plung'd in miry ponds, he gasping lies,
Mud choaks his mouth, and plaisters o'er his eyes.

Of ballad-
singers.

  Let not the ballad-singer's shrilling strain
Amid the swarm thy list'ning ear detain:
Guard well thy pocket; for these *syrens* stand,
To aid the labours of the diving hand;
Confed'rate in the cheat, they draw the throng,
And *cambrick* handkerchiefs reward the song.
But soon as coach or cart drives rattling on,
The rabble part, in shoals they backward run.
So *Jove*'s loud bolts the mingled war divide,
And *Greece* and *Troy* retreats on either side.

Of walking
with a
friend.

  If the rude throng pour on with furious pace,
And hap to break thee from a friend's embrace,
Stop short; nor struggle thro' the croud in vain,
But watch with careful eye the passing train.
Yet I (perhaps too fond) if chance the tide
Tumultuous, bears my partner from my side,
Impatient venture back; despising harm,
I force my passage where the thickest swarm.
Thus his lost bride the *Trojan* sought in vain
Through night, and arms, and flames, and
    hills of slain.
Thus *Nisus* wander'd o'er the pathless grove,
To find the brave companion of his love,
The pathless grove in vain he wanders o'er:
Euryalus alas! is now no more.

That walker, who regardless of his pace,
Turns oft' to pore upon the damsel's face,
From side to side by thrusting elbows tost,
Shall strike his aking breast against the post;
Or water, dash'd from fishy stalls, shall stain
His hapless coat with spirts of scaly rain.
But if unwarily he chance to stray,
Where twirling turnstiles intercept the way,
The thwarting passenger shall force them round,
And beat the wretch half breathless to the ground.

Of inadvertent walkers.

Let constant vigilance thy footsteps guide;
And wary circumspection guard thy side;
Then shalt thou walk unharm'd the dang'rous night,
Nor need th' officious link-boy's smoaky light.
Thou never wilt attempt to cross the road,
Where ale-house benches rest the porter's load,
Grievous to heedless shins; no barrow's wheel,
That bruises oft' the truant school-boy's heel,
Behind thee rolling, with insidious pace,
Shall mark thy stocking with a miry trace.
Let not thy vent'rous steps approach too nigh,
Where gaping wide, low steepy cellars lie;
Should thy shoe wrench aside, down, down you fall,
And overturn the scolding huckster's stall,
The scolding huckster shall not o'er thee moan,
But pence exact for nuts and pears o'erthrown.

Useful precepts.

Safety first of all to be consider'd.

Though you through cleanlier allies wind by day,
To shun the hurries of the publick way,
Yet ne'er to those dark paths by night retire;
Mind only safety, and contemn the mire.
Then no impervious courts thy haste detain,
Nor sneering ale-wives bid thee turn again.

The danger of crossing a square by night.

Where *Lincoln's Inn*, wide space, is rail'd around,
Cross not with vent'rous step; there oft' is found
The lurking thief, who while the day-light shone,
Made the walls echo with his begging tone:
That crutch which late compassion mov'd shall wound
Thy bleeding head, and fell thee to the ground.
Though thou art tempted by the link-man's call,
Yet trust him not along the lonely wall;
In the mid-way he'll quench the flaming brand,
And share the booty with the pilf'ring band.
Still keep the publick streets, where oily rays
Shot from the crystal lamp, o'erspread the ways.

The happiness of London.

Happy *Augusta!* Law-defended town!
Here no dark lanthorns shade the villain's frown;
No *Spanish* jealousies thy lanes infest,
Nor *Roman* vengeance stabs th' unwary breast;
Here *tyranny* ne'er lifts her purple hand,
But liberty and justice guard the land;
No *bravos* here profess the bloody trade,
Nor is the church the murd'rer's refuge made.

    Let not the chairman, with assuming stride,
Press near the wall, and rudely thrust thy side:
The laws have set him bounds; his servile feet
Should ne'er encroach where posts defend the street.
Yet who the footman's arrogance can quell,
Whose flambeau gilds the sashes of *Pall-mall?*
When in long rank a train of torches flame,
To light the midnight visits of the dame?
Others, perhaps, by happier guidance led,
May where the chairmen rests, with safety tread;
Whene'er I pass, their poles unseen below,
Make my knee tremble with the jarring blow.

    If wheels bar up the road, where streets are crost,   *Of crossing*
With gentle words the coachman's ear accost: *the street.*
He ne'er the threat, or harsh command obeys,
But with contempt the spatter'd shoe surveys.
Now man with utmost fortitude thy soul,
To cross the way where carts and coaches roll;
Yet do not in thy hardy skill confide,
Nor rashly risque the kennel's spacious stride;
Stay till afar the distant wheel you hear,
Like dying thunder in the breaking air;
Thy foot will slide upon the miry stone,
And passing coaches crush thy tortur'd bone,
Or wheels enclose the road; on either hand
Pent round with perils, in the midst you stand,
And call for aid in vain; the coachman swears,
And carmen drive, unmindful of thy prayers.

Where wilt thou turn? ah! whither wilt thou fly?
On ev'ry side the pressing spokes are nigh.
So sailors, while *Charybdis'* gulf they shun,
Amaz'd, on *Scylla*'s craggy dangers run.

Of oysters.

Be sure observe where brown *Ostrea* stands,
Who boasts her shelly ware from *Wallfleet* sands;
There may'st thou pass, with safe unmiry feet,
Where the rais'd pavement leads athwart the street.
If where *Fleet-ditch* with muddy current flows,
You chance to roam; where oyster-tubs in rows
Are rang'd beside the posts; there stay thy haste,
And with the sav'ry fish indulge thy taste:
The damsel's knife the gaping shell commands,
While the salt liquor streams between her hands.

The man had sure a palate cover'd o'er
With brass or steel, that on the rocky shore
First broke the oozy oyster's pearly coat,
And risqu'd the living morsel down his throat.
What will not lux'ry taste? earth, sea, and air
Are daily ransacked for the bill of fare.
Blood stuff'd in skins is *British* Christian's food,
And *France* robs marshes of the croaking brood;
Spungy *morels* in strong *ragouts* are found,
And in the *soup* the slimy snail is drown'd.

Observations concerning keeping the wall.

When from high spouts the dashing torrents fall,
Ever be watchful to maintain the wall;
For should'st thou quit thy ground, the rushing throng

Will with impetuous fury drive along;
All press to gain those honours thou hast lost,
And rudely shove thee far without the post.
Then to retrieve the shed you strive in vain,
Draggled all o'er, and soak'd in floods of rain.
Yet rather bear the show'r, and toils of mud,
Than in the doubtful quarrel risque thy blood.

O think on *Œdipus'* detested state,
And by his woes be warn'd to shun thy fate.
Where three roads join'd, he met his sire
    unknown;
(Unhappy sire, but more unhappy son!)
Each claim'd the way, their swords the strife decide,
The hoary monarch fell, he groan'd and dy'd!
Hence sprung the fatal plague that thinn'd thy reign,
Thy cursed incest! and thy children slain!
Hence wert thou doom'd in endless night to stray
Through *Theban* streets, and cheerless groap thy way.

Contemplate, mortal, on thy fleeting years;   *Of a funeral.*
See, with black train the funeral pomp appears!
Whether some heir attends in sable state,
And mourns with outward grief a parent's fate;
Or the fair virgin, nipt in beauty's bloom,
A croud of lovers follow to her tomb.
Why is the herse with 'scutcheons blazon'd round,
And with the nodding plume of ostrich crown'd?
No: the dead know it not, nor profit gain;
It only serves to prove the living vain.

43

How short is life! how frail is human trust!
Is all this pomp for laying 'dust to dust'?

*Of avoiding
paint.*

Where the nail'd hoop defends the painted stall,
Brush not thy sweeping skirt too near the wall;
Thy heedless sleeve will drink the colour'd oil,
And spot indelible thy pocket soil.
Has not wise Nature strung the legs and feet
With firmest nerves, design'd to walk the street?
Has she not given us hands, to groap aright,
Amidst the frequent dangers of the night?
And think'st thou not the double nostril meant,
To warn from oily woes by previous scent?

*Of various
cheats formerly
in practice.*

Who can the various city frauds recite,
With all the petty rapines of the night?
Who now the *guinea-dropper*'s bait regards,
Trick'd by the sharper's dice, or juggler's cards?
Why shou'd I warn thee ne'er to join the fray,
Where the sham-quarrel interrupts the way?
Lives there in these our days so soft a clown,
Brav'd by the bully's oaths, or threat'ning frown?
I need not strict enjoyn the pocket's care,
When from the crouded *play* thou lead'st the fair;
Who has not here, or watch, or snuff-box lost,
Or handkerchiefs that *India*'s shuttle boast?

*An admonition
to virtue.*

O! may thy virtue guard thee through the roads
Of *Drury*'s mazy courts, and dark abodes,
The harlots' guileful paths, who nightly stand,

Where *Katherine-street* descends into the *Strand*.
Say, vagrant Muse, their wiles and subtil arts,
To lure the stranger's unsuspecting hearts;
So shall our youth on healthful sinews tread,
And city cheeks grow warm with rural red.

'Tis she who nightly strowls with saunt'ring pace,
No stubborn stays her yielding shape embrace;
Beneath the lamp her tawdry ribbons glare,
The new-scour'd manteau, and the slattern air;
High-draggled petticoats her travels show,
And hollow cheeks with artful blushes glow;
With flatt'ring sounds she sooths the cred'lous ear,
'My noble captain! charmer! love! my dear!'
In riding-hood, near tavern-doors she plies,
Or muffled pinners hide her livid eyes.
With empty bandbox she delights to range,
And feigns a distant errand from the *'change*;
Nay, she will oft' the Quaker's hood profane,
And trudge demure the rounds of *Drury-lane*.
She darts from sarsnet ambush wily leers,
Twitches thy sleeve, or with familiar airs,
Her fan will pat thy cheek; these snares disdain,
Nor gaze behind thee, when she turns again.

I knew a yeoman, who for thirst of gain,
To the great city drove from *Devon*'s plain
His num'rous lowing herd; his herds he sold,
And his deep leathern pocket bagg'd with gold;
Drawn by a fraudful nymph, he gaz'd, he sigh'd;

*How to know
a whore.*

*A dreadful
example.*

Unmindful of his home, and distant bride,
She leads the willing victim to his doom,
Through winding alleys to her cobweb-room.
Thence thro' the street he reels, from post to post,
Valiant with wine, nor knows his treasure lost.
The vagrant wretch th' assembled watchmen spies,
He waves his hanger, and their poles defies;
Deep in the round-house pent, all night he snores,
And the next morn in vain his fate deplores.
Ah hapless swain, unus'd to pains and ills!
Canst thou forgo roast-beef for nauseous pills?
How wilt thou lift to Heav'n the eyes and hands,
When the long scroll the surgeon's fees demands!
Or else (ye gods avert that worst disgrace)
Thy ruin'd nose falls level with thy face,
Then shall thy wife thy loathsome kiss disdain,
And wholesome neighbours from thy mug refrain.

Of watchmen.
Yet there are watchmen, who with friendly light,
Will teach thy reeling steps to tread aright;
For *sixpence* will support thy helpless arm,
And home conduct thee, safe from nightly harm;
But if they shake their lanthorns, from afar,
To call their brethren to confed'rate war,
When rakes resist their powr; if hapless you
Should chance to wander with the scow'ring crew;
Though Fortune yield thee captive, ne'er despair,
But seek the constable's consid'rate ear;
He will reverse the watchman's harsh decree,
Mov'd by the rhet'rick of a silver fee.

Thus would you gain some fav'rite courtier's word;
Fee not the petty clarks, but bribe my lord.

Now is the time that rakes their revels keep;   *Of rakes.*
Kindlers of riot, enemies of sleep.
His scatter'd pence the flying *Nicker** flings,
And with the copper show'r the casement rings.
Who has not heard the *Scowrer*'s midnight fame?
Who has not trembled at the *Mohock*'s name?
Was there a watchman took his hourly rounds,
Safe from their blows, or new-invented wounds?
I pass their desp'rate deeds, and mischiefs done,
Where from *Snow-hill* black steepy torrents run;
How matrons, hoop'd within the hogshead's womb,
Were tumbled furious thence, the rolling tomb
O'er the stones thunders, bounds from side to side.
So *Regulus* to save his country dy'd.

Where a dim gleam the paly lanthorn throws   *A necessary*
O'er the mid' pavement; heapy rubbish grows,   *caution in a*
Or arched vaults their gaping jaws extend,   *dark night.*
Or the dark caves to common sewers descend.
Oft' by the winds, extinct the signal lies,
Or smother'd in the glimm'ring socket dies,
E'er night has half roll'd round her ebon throne;
In the wide gulph the shatter'd coach o'erthrown,
Sinks with the snorting steeds; the reins are broke,
And from the cracking axle flies the spoke.

*   *Gentlemen, who delighted to break windows with* halfpence.

So when fam'd *Eddystone*'s far-shooting ray,
That led the sailor through the stormy way,
Was from its rocky roots by billows torn,
And the high turret in the whirlewind born,
Fleets bulg'd their sides against the craggy land,
And pitchy ruines blacken'd all the *Strand*.

Who then through night would hire the
    harness'd steed,
And who would choose the rattling wheel for speed?

A fire.   But hark! distress with screaming voice draws
    nigh'r,
And wakes the slumb'ring street with cries of 'fire!'
At first a glowing red enwraps the skies,
And born by winds the scatt'ring sparks arise;
From beam to beam, the fierce contagion spreads;
The spiry flames now lift aloft their heads,
Through the burst sash a blazing deluge pours,
And splitting tiles descend in rattling show'rs.
Now with thick crouds th' enlighten'd pavement
    swarms,
The fire-man sweats beneath his crooked arms,
A leathern casque his vent'rous head descends,
Boldly he climbs where thickest smoak ascends;
Mov'd by the mother's streaming eyes and pray'rs,
The helpless infant through the flame he bears,
With no less virtue, than through hostile fire,
The *Dardan* hero bore his aged sire.
See forceful engines spout their levell'd streams,

To quench the blaze that runs along the beams;
The grappling hook plucks rafters from the walls,
And heaps on heaps the smoaky ruine falls.
Blown by strong winds the fiery tempest roars,
Bears down new walls, and pours along the floors:
The heaven's are all a-blaze, the face of night
Is cover'd with a sanguine dreadful light;
'Twas such a light involv'd thy tow'rs, O *Rome,*
The dire presage of mighty *Cæsar's* doom,
When the sun veil'd in rust his mourning head,
And frightful prodigies the skies o'erspread.
Hark! the drum thunders! far, ye crouds, retire:
Behold! the ready match is tipt with fire,
The nitrous store is laid, the smutty train
With running blaze awakes the barrell'd grain;
Flames sudden wrap the walls; with sullen sound,
The shatter'd pile sinks on the smoaky ground.
So when the years shall have revolv'd the date,
Th' inevitable hour of *Naples'* fate,
Her sapp'd foundations shall with thunders shake,
And heave and toss upon the sulph'rous lake;
Earth's womb at once the fiery flood shall rend,
And in th' abyss her plunging tow'rs descend.

Consider, reader, what fatigues I've known,
The toils, the perils of the wintry Town;
What riots seen, what bustling crouds I bor'd,
How oft' I cross'd where carts and coaches roar'd;
Yet shall I bless my labours, if mankind
Their future safety from my dangers find.

Thus the bold traveller, inur'd to toil,
Whose steps have printed *Asia*'s desert soil,
The barb'rous *Arabs* haunt; or shiv'ring crost
Dark *Greenland*'s mountains of eternal frost;
Whom Providence, in length of years, restores
To the wish'd harbour of his native shores;
Sets forth his journals to the publick view,
To caution, by his woes, the wand'ring crew.

And now compleat my gen'rous labours lye,
Finish'd and ripe for immortality.
Death shall entomb in dust this mould'ring frame,
But never reach th' eternal part, my fame.
When *W*— and *G*—, mighty names, are dead;
Or but at *Chelsea* under custards read;
When criticks crazy bandboxes repair,
And tragedies, turn'd rockets, bounce in air;
High-rais'd on *Fleet-street* posts, consign'd to fame,
This work shall shine, and walkers bless my name.

FINIS

Index.

51

Index

55

Index